D1624935

IS GOD REALLY GOOD?

DESTINY IMAGE BOOKS BY BILL
JOHNSON

God Is Good

Friendship with God

Hosting the Presence

Hosting the Presence Every Day

When Heaven Invades Earth

The Supernatural Power of the Transformed Mind

Strengthen Yourself in the Lord

Releasing the Spirit of Prophecy

Dreaming with God

Here Comes Heaven

Release the Power of Jesus

The Supernatural Ways of Royalty

Spiritual Java

A Life of Miracles

Center of the Universe

Dream Journal

Bill Johnson Answers Your Toughest Questions
About the Goodness of God

IS GOD REALLY GOOD?

BILL JOHNSON

DESTINY IMAGE® PUBLISHERS, INC.
P.O. Box 310, Shippensburg, PA 17257-0310
"Promoting Inspired Lives."

This book and all other Destiny Image and Destiny Image Fiction books are available at Christian bookstores and distributors worldwide.

Cover design by Christian Rafetto
Interior design by Terry Clifton

For more information on foreign distributors, call 717-532-3040.

Reach us on the Internet: www.destinyimage.com.

ISBN 13 HC: 978-0-7684-1611-4
ISBN 13 eBook: 978-0-7684-1622-0
ISBN 13 LP: 978-0-7684-1925-2

For Worldwide Distribution, Printed in the U.S.A.
2 3 4 5 6 7 8 / 21 20 19 18 17

PUBLISHER'S NOTE: *Is God Really Good* is based upon exclusive interview sessions conducted with Pastor Bill Johnson, where people were given the opportunity to ask tough questions about the goodness of God.

CONTENTS

INTRODUCTION

What you believe about the goodness of God determines everything. It actually defines your destiny. But for so many of us, His goodness comes with a question mark. Is God *really* good?

In this short book, I ask Bill Johnson, author of *God is Good: He's Better Than You Think,* a series of hard-to-answer questions about the goodness of God. Will this book answer every theological question you have? No. But it will give you an anchor, and it will answer the most important question that all of us ask: is He *really* good? I believe you will walk away knowing in your heart that yes—yes, He is good.

If it isn't established that God is good, we live with a degree of uncertainty. We approach prayer with more uncertainty than authority. *Is He good?* We live in response to this theological cornerstone.

I love one of Pastor Bill's quotes: "You can't exaggerate His goodness." That is absolutely true. But Pastor Bill also qualifies that statement because, sadly, sometimes we end up distorting His goodness. We can take it to levels that are unbiblical. Truths that have the most prominence and the most importance are the ones that end up coming under attack. They are the ones that end up having counterfeits attached to them. But when we live under the influence of this truth that God is good, how we pray, how we interact with people, how we interact with conflict, and how we interact with our circumstances—all of these things shift dramatically.

I pray specifically that as you read this book and go about your daily life, God will usher you into a divine encounter with His goodness. May His goodness be more than a concept to you—may it be an experience.

LARRY SPARKS
Publisher, Destiny Image

CHAPTER 1

Focusing on God's Goodness in Times of Crisis

We hear so many news reports of terrorism and disaster these days. How do you respond when you watch the news or hear a negative news report? What would you do?

BJ: The first thing is to pray. We can't underestimate the power of prayer. We have to pray, but we have to pray with authority. We have to pray with compassion, which gives us a real root of authority. We're not "begging" God or talking to Him as though He caused the problem. We don't need to persuade Him to do something about it. We're simply standing in positions of authority, saying, "God, this is not okay in my country. This is not okay in my city."

In the Old Testament, if a murder took place out in the wilderness, they would measure the distance to the closest city, and that city had responsibility for it.

What an incredible picture! The responsibility isn't guilt and shame. No, the responsibility is, "God, we need to find a solution for this."

When we see these horrific events taking place, first, we can't become callous to them. Also, we can't move in a soulish way—that is, just out of pity. I don't want to respond in pity or sympathy, because those things aren't okay. Sympathy leaves a person in a problem, but compassion pulls him out. Jesus was moved with compassion. Wherever He was, people were always healed. So learn how to quiet your heart in the midst of conflict and crisis.

• • •

Oftentimes we live in reaction to the devil instead of in response to the Father.

• • •

My wife does this brilliantly. In the middle of a crisis, she will quiet her heart until she comes to a place of real rest and real peace, which sometimes seems impossible to do. The key is just to get with the Lord. You quiet your heart, and then you ask Him, "What are You doing in this situation?"

● ● ●

Sympathy leaves a person in a problem, but compassion pulls him out.

● ● ●

Oftentimes we live in reaction to the devil instead of in response to the Father. Jesus modeled something completely different, and I don't think we're going to get this until we learn how to do what the Father is doing, how to pick up His heartbeat for something.

To be honest, sometimes you'll be praying and the Lord will give you a very specific direction. Maybe what He shows you will help law enforcement to find the person who caused the problem. You could receive any number of things. But the point is that God has an answer, and as long as I am in panic mode, I am a great distance from the breakthrough. So I find a place of rest, find out what He's doing, and pray.

●　●　●

God has an answer. Find out what He's doing, and pray.

●　●　●

CHAPTER 2

HELPING OTHERS SEE GOD'S GOODNESS IN THE MIDST OF PAIN

How do you minister God's goodness to friends or family who are going through difficult times?

BJ: Friends and family are the hardest. I half-jokingly tell people, "You know, a prophet is without honor in his hometown." We know that, which is why God has all of us learn how to minister at home first, so that we do it without honor or the applause of people. If we can learn to do it *without* applause, we can be trusted *with* applause.

But how do we do it with family and friends? Somehow, we get to a place where familiarity doesn't change how we pray. We can be over-familiar with the person, which causes us to pray differently, and we end up praying wrong. It would be easy in some situations to pray with accusation instead of praying for mercy. Sometimes when we know the person well, it is easy to find reasons to accuse them, but if we didn't know them at all, we'd be praying for mercy.

Jesus ministered in Nazareth, and it's a bizarre story, but *"He could do no mighty works there except for a few healings because of their unbelief."* The unbelief was based on familiarity. It's possible to know Jesus the wrong way, and sometimes we can know the people around us the wrong way until we don't recognize who they are in God, and we completely miss an opportunity to draw from what God has put in their lives. This can happen when we minister to people, too. The main thing is to serve well.

• • •

**If we can learn to serve
without applause, we can be
trusted with applause.**

• • •

I had a friend who was going through a bizarre situation with their family and was being accused of the most ridiculous things that are the opposite of who this person is. But if they can weather this without resentment, they will come through with such strength that the family will come to them and feed from them in the years to come. Sometimes we just hold on. We stay faithful and make sure that we love. If we have to protect ourselves, we set boundaries. We don't have to listen to everything that is said. We aren't required to allow people to walk on us. We set some boundaries and follow them well for our own well-being, but we love and serve these people. We pray when we get a chance. If there's a crisis, we pray for them. We pray for them in person if they will allow us to, and if they don't, we pray at home.

CHAPTER 3

GOD'S GOODNESS IN THE OLD TESTAMENT

Can you expand on God's goodness in the Old Testament? Specifically, is it still hard to see God's goodness in the midst of what would look like God killing people, threatening curses as punishment, disobedience, and similar things?

BJ: I think the revelation of God's goodness is all through the Old Testament. In fact, the statement *"The Lord is good"* is in the Old Testament. It's in Nahum 1:7. How many times the Psalms talk about the goodness of the Lord! So it's everywhere. In Ezekiel 33:11, God says He *"takes no delight in the death of the sinner."* So we find God's heart. All the way through, there is no personal pleasure in the death of sinners. He is not angrily vindicating Himself and destroying people. That's not what we see at all. We just see the absence of an answer.

● ● ●

**The revelation of God's goodness
is all through the Old Testament.**

● ● ●

In Ezekiel 22:30, He says, *"I sought for
a man to stand in the gap."* Picture a walled
city and a hole in the wall. What you want
in that situation is soldiers to stand in that
gap. Why? Because if there's an attack,
that's where the attack is going to come—
where the hole is. The walls speak of the
moral integrity of a person's life, and sometimes there are weaknesses and failures and
that sort of stuff, which creates holes in
life. We have family members who really
are open to all kinds of demonic assault.
God is looking for someone to stand in
the gap. He's looking for somebody who
will stand in that open place and plead for
the case of the person who is inviting evil
to come and destroy. He's looking. He's

wanting someone to say, "God, don't bring judgment here. Please show them the same mercy You showed me." He's looking for that. His goodness is all through the Old Testament, and I remind you, Jesus came in the Old Testament. The announcement of a new season started with an angelic presence that showed up and said, *"Glory to God in the highest and on earth peace and goodwill towards men."* It was the pronouncement that the season had shifted and changed. Let's demonstrate and see the glory of God, which is the goodness of God. I just think it's everywhere. I think it's all through Scripture.

CHAPTER 4

DOES THE OLD TESTAMENT STILL APPLY?

In your book, God is Good: He's Better Than You Think, you talked about what passed through the cross and what stopped at the cross. Is there still a place for any aspects of the Old Testament, like the Ten Commandments? Do certain aspects of the law still have applicability in our lives today?

BJ: The Ten Commandments are vital. We cannot say we're under grace and then commit adultery, saying, "Well, we're not under the law anymore." No, that's just stupid. Jesus summarized all the Commandments in loving God first and loving people as ourselves. Here's the deal. When we do that, all the stuff on the list is taken care of. When we serve God, love Him completely, love our neighbor as ourselves, there's not going to be a violation. There's not going to be stealing, lust, or the other junk that goes on in people's lives. That is our approach to the Commandments that God has given us.

* * *

Jesus summarized all the Commandments in loving God first and loving people as ourselves.

* * *

I think we listen to all of them pretty well—we don't lust, we don't steal, and we don't do all these things, but I think probably the most overlooked one of the Ten Commandments is keeping the Sabbath. Keeping the Sabbath is the one that people take advantage of, and it's just as important. We do what He said. Even God rested, so it might be important for us to rest! We take a day where we rest. We let our body recuperate and recover, and we do things that replenish us. Recreation.

Re-create. It's important that we protect that time of rest because it's as vital as our time of work.

CHAPTER 5

An Inside Look at the message, *God is Good*

I would like you to share about how your book, God is Good, *came to be. How did you feel motivated to write this message?*

BJ: The way I write varies from book to book. If somebody gives me a suggestion for a book, I take it before the Lord and I pray, and He confirms it or denies it. I've had kind of a dream in my heart develop and I start writing, and He seems to breathe on it, but this one is completely different. I was in a pastors' meeting/prayer meeting, and while we were praying and just giving testimony of what was happening in our region, I felt like the Lord actually interrupted my thoughts, interrupted everything that was going on in the room, and said, "I want you to write a book about My goodness." And it arrested me. It really shocked me because it wasn't like I had a thought He confirmed.

It was like He interrupted something else and brought the subject up.

• • •

The bottom line is my appeal to people to learn to get a theological cornerstone of God's goodness so firmly intact that the questions that are unanswered never undermine what you do know about His goodness.

• • •

So I made a mental note that this was what I needed to do, put it on my list, and just started to pray into it, started to gather information, and started trying to cultivate and bring to the surface the things that He had been showing me in recent years about His goodness. So that really was the motivation, and I love the subject, and I loved writing on it. But it's such a vast subject that if it were up to me, I would probably wait far too long to write it because I would wait for more questions to be answered than what I can offer. But the bottom line is my appeal to people, which is to learn to get a cornerstone of thought—a theological cornerstone—of God's goodness so firmly intact that the questions that are unanswered never undermine what you do know about His goodness. That's kind of the main deal. The main deal is, here are the questions and the challenges that we have in life—let's not give these the power to undermine what the Lord has shown us about His goodness. That's the process.

What is your favorite aspect about the God is Good message and/or book?

BJ: It was getting the book finished! It was a process. I think I especially liked writing and presenting the first chapter because I just tried to be as kindly confrontational as I can be. I think one of the main keys of the message of *God is Good* is that Jesus Christ is perfect theology. I'd have to see the chapter titles in front of me to pick one, but it's like picking your favorite child, you know. You can't do that. It's not legal. I love all my kids equally.

● ● ●

Jesus Christ is perfect theology.

● ● ●

CHAPTER 6

A Secret About Grace

One of the more controversial aspects that we all deal with today is the idea of hyper-grace, where people use the grace of God as a license to sin. So how would you answer if somebody said, Since God is good, that means I can live any kind of lifestyle I want, right?

BJ: Real grace is hyper-grace. I mean that it is extreme. It's scandalous. It's so perfect and so glorious. It is wonderful—but where I draw the line and say, "Stop it," is where people will use the subject of grace to say they can do what they want because they'll be forgiven. Anyone who thinks that is grace does not see it, and they are in great, great danger. Here's the deal with grace. Look at the Old Testament. The Old Testament says, *"Do not commit adultery."* Jesus, under grace, says, *"Don't lust."* The New Testament is harder. It is much more challenging. The Old Testament says, *"Don't murder."* Jesus comes along and says, *"Don't call your brother a name."* Well, I've had no problem not killing people, but I have called a few names. What's harder? Grace. Why is grace harder? Because in the law you're required, but under grace you're enabled.

**In the law you're required.
Under grace you're enabled.**

Under law we are required to perform. Under grace it's the Spirit of God that enables us to accomplish what we couldn't accomplish otherwise. Grace enables us to do what only Jesus can do. So hyper-grace? Real grace is hyper, and it'll make you hyper, but grace never empowers us to sin. It always empowers us to obey the Lord.

CHAPTER 7

GOD'S DISCIPLINE AND NON-BELIEVERS

You've said before that God disciplines the Church to purify them, causing revival outside of the Church. Does God ever discipline non-believers?

BJ: Yes, of course. He can do anything He wants. I mean, He's God. None of what I teach confines Him. It's just to get us to understand His heart and what He's like. Yes, He can discipline anybody He wants. In fact, I think you see it all the time. The scary one is Herod in the New Testament. Herod is standing before a group of people and giving a speech, and the people are so moved by the speech that they start crying out, *"The voice of a God and not a man, the voice of a God and not a man"* (see Acts 12:22). And it says the angel of the Lord killed him. That's pretty good discipline—the angel killed him because he didn't give glory to God. Now reason through this. He didn't give glory to God, which has to imply God was responsible for anointing his speech so that he could move a crowd and have that kind of favor. It was a gift from God, but because God gave him an extreme gift, and he had no recognition of God in the gift, it cost him.

I think God does discipline non-believers. Pharaoh is another good one. The Lord reached out to Pharaoh time and time and time again. It was only after constant rejection of what God was bringing that we see His judgment on Pharaoh. When God disciplines, it always ends in a judgment. What He wants is for them to be saved. Anyway, that's not a complete answer; it's just part.

CHAPTER 8

God's Heart
Concerning
Poverty

What is God's heart concerning financial poverty? Should we stand against poverty as believers, and if so, how does that affect being content in all circumstances?

BJ: Poverty is not spiritual. Honor it only if it is in Heaven. Is there any lack up there? No, there isn't.

● ● ●

Jesus promises that He will give back a hundred times what you left.

● ● ●

The Lord's Prayer says, *"Deliver us from evil"* (Matt 6:13). That word *evil* comes from a word that means "physical pain," which comes from a root word that means "poor." So we have *evil*, "sin"; we have *pain*, "sickness"; and we have *poor*, "poverty." The redemptive touch of Jesus was supposed to touch all three areas—our prosperity is supposed to matter to us. The Scripture says that God *"...has delight in the prosperity of His servant"* (Ps. 35:27). I know there have been branches of the Church that have, at times, exalted and honored poverty as a rite of passage, so to speak, thinking that this is how you come into great faith. I don't think it's right. I think it's wrong. I understand that many have pursued prosperity and have become independent, arrogant, and everything else that Jesus didn't teach, so I understand that there's great difficulty that comes with increased finances, but it's not automatic. In fact, let me put it this way. Peter says to Jesus in Mark 10:28, *"...we have left all and followed You."* And Jesus says, "That's right. That's good, and I'm going to return whatever people have left behind; I'm going to return a hundred times as much in this life plus life in the age to come." Jesus promises that He will give back a hundred times what you left. Think through this. It's like Jesus is holding up money and He says, "See this stuff? It'll kill you. Now if you leave it for My sake, I'm going to give you a hundred times as much of what will kill you." The whole point is that when we have made the decision to serve Him and Him only, He can trust us with the blessing. *Seek first the kingdom of God and His righteousness, and all these things shall be added to you* (Matt. 6:33). If we seek first what needs to be added, we miss both. Prosperity isn't necessarily spiritual; poverty isn't necessarily spiritual. This is my hot button. This is what I want to talk about to free people from poverty.

CHAPTER 9

WHEN YOU DON'T SEE HEALING

Could you expand on your personal journey of moving from guilt and shame when somebody doesn't get healed and when you don't see a breakthrough? How did you react then versus how you react now?

BJ: I would quit praying for people. If somebody would come and want prayer, I would have them go to somebody else, or I would pray a token prayer just to get them out of my way. We get discouraged and we think, *I've got guns but they're not loaded.* There's nothing there to help in the situation. What guilt and shame does is, it takes our focus from the One it's supposed to be on to the one it's not supposed to be on. We have to learn how to maneuver with pain and loss—not away from God, but to Him until we have that sense of presence, and we're unwilling to change our assignment according to how we feel or according to our track record. That's the hardest thing to do. How do we maintain the call of God on our life when we've just experienced the greatest loss in our life? What do we do? We have to find someone to pray for.

●　●　●

What guilt and shame does is it takes our focus from the One it's supposed to be on to the one it's not supposed to be on.

●　●　●

I remember when Eric, my oldest, was in Weaverville. We got a phone call telling us he was barely breathing. He had gotten hit with an asthmatic thing. Candace, his wife, could hardly see his chest moving at all, and they rushed him to the hospital. It was a Sunday morning. Beni and I ran up there. We prayed and the Lord really touched him, and we were grateful. I came back down here in time for the second service and had an altar call for everybody who had breathing problems—we have to go after this stuff. We have to look for the problem. We can't just say, "Well, I have no anointing there." We can't say, "Well, it's just life." No, it's not life—it's death, and it doesn't belong in the Kingdom, and we have to do what we know to do. Sometimes we get the breakthrough, and we give Him the glory. Sometimes we don't, and we get back into prayer and go after it again. I don't know any other way.

● ● ●

Sometimes we get the breakthrough, and we give Him the glory. Sometimes we don't, and we get back into prayer and go after the breakthrough again.

● ● ●

CHAPTER 10

God's Goodness and the Power of Hope

How is hope related to understanding the goodness of God? How does a revelation of God's goodness fuel our hope?

BJ: We can't see His goodness and not be filled with hope. If we can imagine His goodness is bigger than space itself, and we get a little glimpse of that, we will feel pretty foolish to be hopeless. What is there that's so large in my life that His goodness does not completely envelope and take under wraps, under rule, under control, under influence?

● ● ●

We can't see His goodness and not be filled with hope.

● ● ●

I think hope is one of the most important elements of influence we are supposed to have. In fact, one of our women in the church said the Lord told her that the person with the most hope will always have the most influence. That's become kind of a standard statement around here for the last several years. "The person with the most hope will always have the most influence." We can't see the goodness of God and not have hope, so if we don't have hope, better take a good look. We consider prayerfully and meditate on the passages of Scripture that talk about hope. Psalm 27:13 says, *"I would have lost heart* (hope), *unless I had believed that I would see the goodness of the Lord In the land of the living."* We have so much reason to hope—to the point where we become contagious in hope. We infect people with our hope, and I think anybody who sees the goodness of God continuously will have nothing flowing out of their life but hope.

● ● ●

I think anybody who sees the goodness of God continuously will have nothing flowing out of their life but hope.

● ● ●

CHAPTER 11

GOD'S GLORY AND HIS GOODNESS

In the story of Moses asking to see God's glory, is there a difference between His glory and His goodness, or are they the same thing?

BJ: *"Moses said, 'Now show me your glory.' And the Lord said, 'I will cause all my goodness to pass in front of you'"* (see Exod. 33.18). I think the Lord's response to Moses implies that they're one and the same. Maybe I would say it this way: they are two sides of the same coin. One is connected to the other. You can't separate the two—the goodness of God, the glory. I've always looked at the glory as the eminence, the emanating presence of God, but when God revealed it according to Moses' request, He said, *"This is what you're going to see."* I just don't think you can separate the two. I think they are so

intrinsically one, that they are two sides of
the same coin.

● ● ●

**You can't separate the two—the
goodness of God, the glory. They
are two sides of the same coin.**

● ● ●

CHAPTER 12

How to Inundate Yourself with God's Goodness

What are some things people can do to really feed on the goodness of God and inundate themselves with His goodness?

BJ: The Word of God is what reveals who He is. Don't get caught up in the judgment and destructions of the Old Testament. I'm not saying don't read them, but read them through this filter: "This set the stage for what I get to taste of." Let it create thankfulness. Let it create a context. Yes, sin is severe. No one who sees that would come into a place of embracing grace so they could be empowered to sin. Read the Old Testament, but feed yourself on who Jesus is in the Gospels. If you have any question about what He's like, read the Gospels. Read the Book of Acts. Look at how Jesus responded to loss, how He responded to conflict, how He responded to problems. Prayerfully meditate. Look at the stories. Look at the way He treated the woman who was caught in adultery. There was the absence of vindication. There was the absence of, "I want to show you how wrong you were so that I can show you your need for salvation." He didn't rub her nose in the problem. There's something so gracious about the way He handled this situation.

● ● ●

Sin is severe. No one who sees that would come into a place of embracing grace so they could be empowered to sin.

● ● ●

The demoniac was a man who must have had multiple generations of issues, a lifetime subscription of issues, and yet he comes to Jesus, and with a word, Jesus brings a deliverance. The crazy thing about the story is that it says the people of the city that he came from were afraid because he was clothed and in his right mind. The change was so extreme from what he'd been that they were now nervous. That, to me, is the fear of God being created through goodness.

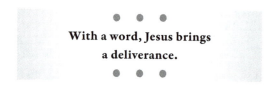

With a word, Jesus brings a deliverance.

Read these stories and learn the art of meditation. Meditation in the world is emptying your mind; biblical meditation is filling your mind. You just fill it with the right thing. How many of us have stayed awake at night worrying about a problem? How many of us couldn't shake something, a thought or something that troubled us, for hours and hours? So we've proven we know how to meditate. We just need to change what we draw up. That is the art of biblical meditation. Take that verse *"I would have despaired."* I would have, but I'm not going to. Why? Because I live with a hope for the goodness of God to be seen where I live.

* * *

Meditation in the world is emptying your mind; biblical meditation is filling your mind.

* * *

Take these Scriptures and prayerfully meditate on them. *"The Lord delights in the prosperity of His servant"* (see Ps. 35:27). Hold that up in front of you in the middle of a financial crisis. Keep that in front of you. Why? Because it keeps hope alive, and as long as hope is alive, you actually attract the activities of Heaven into your life.

Sometimes I think we repel God's solutions by our conversation and actions, so this conviction of the goodness of God is something that we protect no matter what happens. Protect that thing in your heart and don't let anyone rob it. It's greater than you can imagine, so feed on it. Feed on it in song—sing about it. It doesn't have to sound pretty, so do it by yourself. But honestly, sing a fresh song, a new song of His goodness. Quote the Scriptures. Memorize, meditate, talk about His goodness with friends. Get testimonies. Ask your friends, "What is God doing?" Feed yourself, and you'll be infectious in no time.

CHAPTER 13

WHAT YOU
BELIEVE ABOUT
GOD'S GOODNESS
DETERMINES
YOUR DESTINY

How does having the goodness of God solidified in your heart actually determine your destiny concerning God's goodness?

BJ: We are made in His image. If He's not good, who are we? What's our purpose? What's our potential? I mean, if He's not better than we can imagine, then our own destiny is pretty insignificant because the Church tends to think we mirror someone who is always angry. So it justifies inappropriate behavior, and it legitimizes unrighteous reaction to problems. We don't have that right.

● ● ●

If He's not good, who are we? What's our purpose? What's our potential?

● ● ●

Every believer says God is good because it's in the Bible. The Bible declares God is good, so we have to say that, but our definition of His goodness is perfectly defined in Jesus. Jesus modeled it in that every problem He faced, He brought a solution. He didn't say, "Well, just learn to endure. Just learn to adjust your life to this issue, this affliction, or torment." He always brought a redemptive solution. He's illustrating the heart of a perfect Father, and now it's our responsibility and privilege to learn to do the same.

● ● ●

Our definition of God's goodness is perfectly defined in Jesus.

● ● ●

We don't always do it well, but at least if we can get that one issue settled, then we won't constantly have to wrestle with the possibility that God caused the problem or created the affliction, that He empowered the devil to do this. We can settle the issue. We've covered about half the distance to breakthrough right there because we don't have to go over these hurdles every time there's a problem. It's crazy, but people will say, "Well, God gave me the affliction to teach me patience." All right. So why are you going to the doctor? Why do you go to a doctor to get rid of something that God gave you? It's nonsense. We just haven't thought through this stuff.

CHAPTER 14

INTIMACY WITH JESUS

It seems that your understanding of God's goodness was born and developed in your daily time of intimacy with the Lord in the secret place. That looks different for everybody, but what does your daily routine look like?

BJ: My prayer life has changed so much through the years. It used to be very task-oriented in the sense that we need this breakthrough, we need this miracle, we need this open-door for favor. We all have our burdens that we're supposed to pray for. It's our privilege to pray petition prayers. But the bulk of my time with the Lord—at least 75 percent of my time with Him, maybe more—is just in adoration. Now it has changed so much that the bulk of my time is just in that relationship where I express my affection for Him.

● ● ●

**The bulk of my time with the Lord—at
least 75 percent of my time with Him,
maybe more—is just in adoration.**

● ● ●

I like to be engaged. I like to be
embraced, in a sense, with the presence
of the Lord and function from that place.
It's not just during a prayer time in the
morning or at night, but it's throughout
the day where I just pause. I like to turn
my heart of affection toward Him and just
realize His presence. In that, it's a relationship that isn't task-centered. He's with
me always, and I want to become aware
of Him. I want to turn my heart to Him.
That's a huge part of my life. It's the bulk of
it. I have things I go through like everyone
else. I pray throughout the day constantly
and go over the things that I want to see
the Lord do, but if there is anything that

defines my relationship, it is that affection and adoration for Him. That's the bulk of my walk, regardless of what's happening.

CHAPTER 15

TURNING YOUR HEART TOWARD JESUS

What does turning your affection and attention to the Lord look like?

BJ: I've become aware of Him. It's impossible to see Him and not love Him. We turn our focus away from every other barking voice, every other situation that may be appealing or repulsive—it doesn't matter. We separate ourselves from all those things and just focus on the One who loves us most.

● ● ●

It's impossible to see Him and not love Him.

● ● ●

It's becoming aware of Him. It isn't this big mental exercise, although the mind is involved. It's that my heart has affection for Him. I have encountered Him, and I pause and realize that my love for Him in this moment is the most important thing in my life. Then I turn that affection toward Him.

Not having it be agenda-driven is a big deal. It isn't like I want to get close so I can pray about this; He's already here and I get that, but there's something about that awareness of His heart for me and for people. It's just feeling His heart. It changes my perspective on everything, so that's all it is. It's really simple. I become aware of Him, and I turn my affection towards Him. Obviously, I tell Him how much I love Him, and praise and worship is involved in that, but not as an activity; it's just as the most natural response you can imagine.

CHAPTER 16

Is God in Control?

Many of us say, "God is in control." We use that language. But you make a controversial statement. You say that God is in charge, but He's not in control. What can you tell us about this?

BJ: We've developed the "God is in control" language to account for evil. We try to say that He was the God who either caused it or somehow approved it. I struggle with that kind of language, and every parent should be able to relate to this. We are in charge of our household, but we're not in control of everything that happens. There are two words for the will of God in the New Testament. One refers to "that which is concrete;" it's firm, fixed, unchangeable. The other is oftentimes determined by the role that we play.

• • •

**Every parent should be able to
relate to this. We are in charge of
our household, but we're not in
control of everything that happens.**

• • •

Regarding the return of Jesus, we can say "yes" or "no." We don't have to believe it—it's still going to happen. Our belief concerning His return doesn't change it. *"The Lord...is not willing that any should perish"* (2 Pet. 3:9). is perhaps the best example. Are people perishing? Yes. Is it His will? No. Is He in control of that? He's not in control in the sense that He is sponsoring their demise, and His will is for them to end up in eternal punishment. No, that's not His heart. His heart is for everyone to turn to Him. Somehow, we have to settle these issues where we know of His goodness, and we represent it well in the way we treat people who are broken, who are fallen, sometimes who are enemies to the cross. How do we respond to these people? We have the responsibility of representing Him well.

●　●　●

**Are people perishing? Yes.
Is it His will? No.**

●　●　●

Jesus said, *"As the Father has sent Me, I also send you"* (John 20:21). It was the Father, who was perfect, who sent Jesus. Now it's the Father, through Jesus, who sends us to do what? The same things Jesus did, with the exception of the redemptive role of atonement. That alone belongs to the Lamb of God. But we still have the responsibility to display the Father, and He is good. He's not without standards; it isn't that anything goes and He blesses it.

No, that's nonsense. That's not right, but in my love for God, I have to learn to hate what He hates. And He hates affliction. He hates sin. He hates all these things, but He loves sinners, and He loves the afflicted. So we need to learn to navigate through this life to represent His goodness well.

CHAPTER 17

Does God Ever Give Someone a Disease?

It appears that God gives satan permission to torment Job. Is God allowing sickness and destruction, as many people would argue, or is God stating what was true at the time in the context of Job?

BJ: I don't have a good answer. The answer that satisfies my heart is that Jesus represented the Father differently in the New Testament than what was revealed in the Old. Did things change? I don't know, but I'm not a disciple of Job; I'm a disciple of Jesus, and I can't give explanations for all the things that happened in the Old Testament. To me it's all connected to the severity of sin. The Lord is exposing something that the entire Old Testament was about—the severity of sin, the complete lost condition of humanity—and the only possible Savior was this Lamb of God. Everything pointed to that. Once

Jesus comes on the scene, we don't see situations like Job's anymore. We don't see the Father causing anything. If Jesus is rebuking a storm and the Father sent it, then we have a divided house. We have a Son opposed to the Father's purposes. So there is a power behind that storm that is not from God, and Jesus was rebuking it. He wasn't just directing weather; He was dealing with an entity.

● ● ●

**I'm not a disciple of Job;
I'm a disciple of Jesus.**

● ● ●

> *Since God never gives us a disease or sickness to teach us a lesson, why did He allow satan to give Job a disease?*

BJ: The standard in the Old Testament has been replaced with perfect theology. I'm not going to sacrifice sheep, and neither am I going to use Job as an example. Job is the question; Jesus is the answer. There are a lot of these mysteries I can't explain, but I don't feel I need to. I see enough in Jesus to know what to do.

● ● ●

Job is the question; Jesus is the answer.

● ● ●

Think about the whole situation with the Pool of Bethesda where one person was healed. If that happened today, everybody would be interviewing all the people around the pool who didn't get healed, asking them, "How did it feel to have Jesus walk past you?" So much of what we create in our theology today is based on what didn't happen instead of what did. We need to celebrate what God is saying and what He's doing, and that will help us to get greater and greater breakthroughs.

● ● ●

So much of what we create in our theology today is based on what didn't happen instead of what did.

● ● ●

CHAPTER 18

What If Your Prophetic Word Isn't Coming to Pass?

How do you stand on the foundation of God's goodness when you receive a prophetic word and it's not coming to pass? How is God's goodness an anchor in that process?

BJ: Here is something I work very hard to do. The Father spoke to Jesus and called Him His beloved Son. Satan showed up and said, *"If You are the Son of God"* (see Matt. 4:3-6). The devil raised a question to something the Father had spoken to Jesus. What Jesus refused to do was give power to the question to undermine the revelation. The revelation He received was intact. He refused to allow any question to deteriorate the revelation. And we have the same responsibility. When there's a promise that is unfulfilled, we keep it there before us. The Bible says, *"But Mary kept all these things and pondered them in* *her heart"* (Luke 2:19). Mary, the mother of Jesus, had some words about her Son that she pondered that weren't fulfilled for thirty years. She kept them in a safe place, in the womb of her heart, to be nurtured and developed until the time that the Father chose to unveil His purposes.

● ● ●

What Jesus refused to do was give power to question to undermine the revelation.

● ● ●

We can look at Abraham and the word he received. It was decades before there was fulfillment. Sometimes the word comes, and it's within weeks or days; sometimes it's fulfilled within hours. Other times, you just have to wait. So what I do is I put these words on a shelf, and as my heart begins to leap with conviction for one of them, I pull the word off the shelf and I ponder it. I pray into it and confess what I believe God is saying. I will look for a Scripture, or I will ask the Father if there's anything I'm supposed to do. Abraham still had to co-labor with the Lord, so to speak, for Isaac to be born. He still had a role to play. He couldn't bring about a miracle, but he still had a role to play. So I will ask, "Lord, is there something that You want me to do?" That's what I do, and I'll do it for a season. If there's no breakthrough, I'll put it back.

I keep it before me so that I have that hope, knowing that I don't really get the timing of the Lord, but I get to participate.

• • •

If there's no breakthrough, I'll put the word back on the shelf.

• • •

CHAPTER 19

God's Goodness
and the Lost

As Christians, how can we truly love the lost without being offended by their sin?

BJ: It's easier when you realize how completely lost you were. When we pray for cities like San Francisco or New Orleans or whatever, it's very easy to be offended at the sin, and it should bother us in the sense that sin is so devastating, but if we realized how lost we were, we could pray effectively for these cities. We could say, "God, I didn't deserve Your kindness any more than they do, but You showed it to me. You were kind to me. You were merciful. You gave me the gift of repentance, and I'm asking now that You'd give this city the gift of repentance." We pray out of that position.

• • •

You don't ever see Jesus standing before the Father accusing people.

• • •

When Nehemiah prayed over Jerusalem and the restoration of the city and nation, he said, "God, forgive us for we have sinned" (see Neh. 1:6-7). I don't believe he did any of the sins he was confessing, but he so identified with his people in their lost condition that he prayed on their behalf as though their problem was his. And that's really what it takes. It takes so identifying with broken people that we say, "God, we are in need of Your mercy. We are in need." That's what an intercessor is. We stand in the shoes of another and plead their case as though it were our own. When we take that posture, I personally think that's what a priestly ministry is supposed to do. We not only minister to the Lord but also on behalf of people before the Lord. That is the role. You don't ever see Jesus standing before the Father accusing people. He was so free of accusation that sinners wanted to be with Him, and yet He in no way applauded or gave room to sin. They wanted to be with Him because there wasn't that threat of condemnation. Everybody wants to be free of what kills them. They just have to see it for what it is, and we have a chance to illustrate it.

CHAPTER 20

EVANGELISM AND THE VALUE WE PLACE ON OTHERS

*At Bethel, you've removed the dividing line
between an us-and-them kind of language.
Why would you say that's so important?*

BJ: Nobody wants to be our project. I
grew up in a church where evangelism was
a big deal, as it should be. Missions is a big
deal, but who wants to be my project? I
keep spending time with "them" because
I want them to be saved. Is that a noble
reason? Of course, it is. But if they're not
receptive, then we tend to choose to go
somewhere else instead of loving them just
for the privilege of loving them.

● ● ●

**Everybody wants to be valuable to
somebody else just because of who
they are. That's what evangelism
is really supposed to be.
It's supposed to be driven by the value
that we place on people.**

● ● ●

I think people can tell when we have a hidden agenda. It's like being in a multi-level marketing meeting. You got invited over to somebody's house for dinner, and you realize about halfway through the meal it's because they want you to buy something. Nobody likes that. It's manipulation. Everybody wants to be valuable to somebody else just because of who they are. That's what evangelism is really supposed to be. It's supposed to be driven by the value that we place on people.

CHAPTER 21

God's Goodness at Creation

Is the goodness of God reflected in His original intent at creation and in the Garden of Eden?

BJ: He apparently placed Adam and Eve on a planet that was already occupied by the devil. He created a garden that was limited in size, and He told them to be fruitful, multiply, and subdue the earth (see Gen. 1:28.) *Subdue* is military; it's an advancement that increases the size of the garden until the entire planet is ruled over by people made in His image who were His delegated authority. That was His intent.

• • •

Subdue is military; it's an advancement that increases the size of the garden until the entire planet is ruled over by people made in His image who were His delegated authority.

• • •

When sin came, the authority to rule, that key, was handed over to a serpent. When that serpent tempted Jesus after His forty-day fast, he said, *All this authority I will give You, and their glory; for this has been delivered to me, and I give it to whomever I wish"* (Luke 4:5-7). Here's the deal. God created us to be His delegated authority, to illustrate and model His generous, delightful rule over all creation, and when we partnered with the liar, we invited him to afflict us. When Jesus died and rose again, He basically declared, "I got the keys back." He said, *"All authority has been given to Me in heaven and on earth. Go therefore..."* (Matt. 28:18-19. He re-assigned us to the original task.

● ● ●

God created us to be His delegated authority, to illustrate and model His generous, delightful rule over all creation.

● ● ●

CHAPTER 22

ENCOUNTERING
A GOOD GOD

How do you set yourself up for an encounter with God?

BJ: We cry out! We just cry out. We don't control the divine encounter. I think it's important that we pursue God; we cry out to God for more, but we don't require Him in our thinking and in our request to touch us a certain way. He knows exactly what we need, what's going to impact us the most in this moment. It may be something very subtle whose full impact takes months or years for me to realize. I am still living under the influence of the first profound encounter I had like that. He spoke to my heart in May of 1979. I still remember the influence of that touch. I didn't realize how significant it was at the moment, but if I had said, "Well, God I want to shake, fall, rattle, and roll," then I would have disregarded what He was doing. But I just want Him, however He shows up.

●　●　●

If you're not thankful for what you have, you're not ready for more because you're not a good steward of what He has given you. Good stewardship invites increase.

●　●　●

As you pray for an encounter, don't box Him in or tell Him how He's going to do it. Let your longing for Him be a continual ache, but let it be in the context of thankfulness for what you have. You have to press in for more while being thankful for what you have. If you're not thankful for what you have, you're not ready for more because you're not a good steward of what He has given you. Good stewardship invites increase.

What would you say in terms of just encouraging people to yield to the Lord and what He wants the encounter to look like?

BJ: He takes us as we come. If we have impure motives, He's still going to bring us close to Himself, and the impurities will get pruned off. What I don't want to do is have somebody clean the house before He comes to clean the house. We just need to come to Him as we are.

Come as honestly as you know how to be. Be persistent. Be hungry. Be expressive. Realize that one touch from the Lord changes everything. Just don't make it on your terms; make it on His.

The Bible says that when Moses saw the burning bush, he turned aside (see Exod. 3:3-4). He changed his direction and embraced another direction. Sometimes the

Lord will do something subtle that gives us the opportunity to change our focus and direction, and if we just keep going the way we're going and we don't change our focus, we sometimes miss those subtle invitations that He gives us to step aside. The Bible says that when Moses turned aside, the Lord spoke. When he repositioned himself in a different focus, it attracted the voice of the Lord.

●　●　●

The Lord takes us as we come. If we have impure motives, He's still going to bring us close to Himself, and the impurities will get pruned.

●　●　●

CHAPTER 23

DEALING WITH DISAPPOINTMENT

How do you balance processing life events that are disappointing and painful in a healthy way while maintaining the Kingdom perspective that God is good?

BJ: We fill our heart with what God is doing. If we can't see what He's doing, we fill our heart with what He's done. We fill our heart with what He's saying. If we can't hear Him, then we return to what He has said, but we build our heart condition around history with God, His redemptive interventions. We let these things feed our soul. If we feed ourselves on what didn't happen, we will fall into a spirit of offense and eventually into unbelief. We just can't afford to do that, so we have to guard our heart.

• • •

**We fill our heart with what God is
doing. If we can't see what He's doing,
we fill our heart with what He's done.**

• • •

They say the Pool of Bethesda could
have had as many as a thousand people
around it. Jesus healed one person. The
Bible celebrates the one. Much of the
Church writes theology around the 999.
What we can't afford to do is allow what
didn't happen to change our approach to a
good Father. Some things in life we have to
embrace out of our overall trust in Him. I
trust Him—period. I don't have an explanation, but I don't need one to obey. All I
need to know is, "What do I do next?" I can
receive the peace that passes all understanding because I don't insist on understanding.
I give up my right to understand. Therefore,
I can receive peace that goes past it.

● ● ●

**What we can't afford to do is allow
what didn't happen to change
our approach to a good Father.**

● ● ●

The bottom line is, "What is He looking for?" He's looking for trust. He's looking for people who believe Him no matter what. It's easy to believe Him when the bank account is full, everyone you pray for is healed, everybody in your family is healthy, wealthy and wise, and all is well in the world. It's really easy to give Him all the thanks and all the praise, but I can't be trusted with what I've prayed for if I can't navigate my way through disappointment.

• • •

I can't be trusted with what I've prayed for if I can't navigate my way through disappointment.

• • •

We've all prayed the big prayers. We've prayed, "God, we want to see nations changed. We want to see nations come to You. God, I want You to use me to impact these people. I want everyone I pray for to get touched by Your love. I want all cancer that walks through the doors at Bethel Church to dissolve." We pray these big prayers, and it's like He says, "All right. I'm answering that—here's your journey. How do you handle disappointment? Are you going to accuse Me when it doesn't happen like you think? Are you going to withdraw from Me? Are you going to withdraw your love from Me?" I don't think He ever looks at it in a punishment way, but He is measuring us to see the weight of blessing He can put on us that won't crush us. Blessing establishes the sanctified life; it crushes the unsanctified life. If I'm divided in my willingness to trust Him regardless, if I'm divided in that trust, then I've already predetermined how much I can handle, and God in His mercy will keep certain measures of glory away from me because they will crush me. So I think it's the process of just trusting Him regardless.

● ● ●

Blessing establishes the sanctified life; it crushes the unsanctified life.

● ● ●

In early 2016, I had a medical issue that was really quite sobering. One of the things that happened is I came out of it with this conviction that bold faith stands on the shoulders of quiet trust. What He's trying to build in us is this issue of quiet trust. Regardless of how crazy it may look, how crazy it may sound, our trust is absolutely in Him. That lifestyle of quiet trust gives us the platform to stand on when it's time for that bold faith, the bold decree, the aggressive pursuit of this breakthrough.

CHAPTER 24

God's Sovereignty in the Midst of Pain

> *If God is good and we shouldn't blame God when bad things happen, or even say He allowed them to happen, then how do you explain His sovereignty in painful situations?*

BJ: You know He's God. He can do whatever He wants. I would never pretend to know what He always purposes to do, but Jesus gives me a good enough example to follow. You know the point I keep coming back to is what you think about God. If you can't find it in the person of Jesus, you have reason to question it.

• • •

If you can't find it in the person of Jesus, you have reason to question it.

• • •

With a lot of the questions people ask, we may not have all the explanation we want, but the turmoil of the heart is settled when we consider Jesus. How did Jesus handle this? How did He handle that? What did He do in this conflict? What did He do here? He set a standard and He modeled something that we actually can do. If we don't get that peace, then we'll constantly be reinterpreting what we're supposed to do with Jesus out of the picture. We would never go to the church and say, "All right, this weekend we're going to sacrifice sheep because we want to give honor to the Old Testament." We'd never do that. We'd never go back to that. Why? Because Jesus reset the stage, and now the only sacrifice that matters is His. Everything else is in the past. It's a reference point, but it no longer has merit today. Why? Because the Lamb of God came. We have all this stuff going on in the Old Testament that we may not be able to explain, but we do have something very clear that showed up: That is Jesus illustrating the Father. Why redefine Him? Why allow Old Testament experience to trump what Jesus revealed? I just think it's as illogical as sacrificing sheep.

CHAPTER 25

ENGAGING THE POLITICAL REALM

In the political realm, how would you address the goodness of God to the Body of Christ to bring healing from division?

BJ: Don't participate. The political spirit really doesn't care which side of an issue you're on as long as you're angry at somebody, as long as you feel superior to somebody else's opinion. The political spirit is manipulative in nature. It gains through popular vote. It pressures and manipulates people to persuasion. It uses fear and all kinds of intimidating factors to get people to unknowingly participate in it. You just can't afford to do it. You have to spot it for what it is—it's a demonic power. It's humanistic in nature. It is focused on the glory that man is central to everything and not God. Jesus warned us to be careful of the leaven of Herod. That was that political spirit.

● ● ●

The political spirit really doesn't care which side of an issue you're on as long as you're angry at somebody.

● ● ●

The religious spirit isn't any safer. It has God at the center of everything, but He's impersonal and powerless. There's no personal relationship or interaction. Both of those powers—the political spirit and the religious spirit—are working to divide the hearts of men. So, number one, just don't be involved in them. Show compassion to people on both sides of the issues, but pray in private.

● ● ●

Jesus warned us to be careful of the leaven of Herod. That was that political spirit.

● ● ●

We need the Lord to restore discernment. The spirit of offense has caused the Church to lose its discernment of what's actually going on behind the scenes. Unless we know the elected officials, unless we have people "in the know" in these camps, we only know about these people what the media wants us to know. It's carefully picked and projected because they want to shape all of us and our public opinion. What we've got to do is to pray that the Lord Himself would expose and reveal and that we would be able to pray for our government without the spirit of accusation. We've got to pray that God would bring His purposes forth. We have issues; we have abortion issues. These are issues that we have to take to heart and pray for and pray that God would open our eyes so that we are restored to being a people of conviction instead of reaction.

CHAPTER 26

How to Talk to Children About Suffering

How do we put the goodness of God and the tragedy of loss in language that our young children can understand?

BJ: I don't know, except in the people I work with who experience great loss, there is a confidence that God is able to turn the greatest tragedy into a triumph. It's more than a phrase or a statement. It's a reality. In the middle of huge pain and loss, it's impossible to process that. So when there is loss, we need to give time for mourning. We don't want to try to talk people out of it by saying, "Well, God is good. Everything will be okay." We just need to be there for them. We listen, love, ache with them, weep with them. We do whatever we need to do, but in that season of mourning, we need to guard ourselves so that mourning doesn't take us into unbelief, which mourning can do.

● ● ●

We listen, love, ache with them, weep with them.

● ● ●

Mark 16 is a great chapter that shows how mourning took the disciples into unbelief. They heard the testimony of Jesus and they rejected it—until Jesus finally showed up and rebuked them for rejecting the evidence that they were presented with. What set them up for rejecting the evidence? It was mourning. Mourning is legal. *"Blessed are those who mourn. They shall be comforted."* Mourning, when it's done correctly, actually attracts the Holy Spirit into a situation. Proper mourning is good. It's right and fine, so we give place for it. We prayerfully set a protection zone, if you will, around our children as they're sad and as they sorrow, but in the timing of the

Lord, we begin to discern, "All right. Now we need to prepare ourselves for the Lord to redeem the loss and to turn it around." Then we start praying, not as a reaction, but now as a response to the heart of the Father. "God, we ask now that You would bring healing and that You would vindicate the loss." That kind of language helps kids to know the loss is not the end. The loss is in the middle of the story. The end is He redeems it and somehow makes what was meant to destroy us establish and empower us instead. This is a language of hope, and it doesn't have to answer all the questions.

We can't answer all the questions. Why did this happen? I don't know why—but I know He's good enough to trust, and I know that outside of His goodness, I won't find anything I need that will be helpful. All anything else will do is corrupt my heart to be antagonistic or distant toward this loving Father. And so, this goodness of God is what compels me to come. It says, *"It's out of His goodness and kindness that He gives us the gift of repentance"* (see Rom. 2:4). Repentance is the result of seeing His goodness for what it is. Not that repentance is needed in that situation, but the point is turning to God comes out of kindness. So we just always have to keep that in our families in any kind of disappointment or loss. We keep it there in language or conversation—the way we talk, the way we confess our confidence in God. We don't fight to appear reasonable, because that's where we make up stupid answers to problems—because we're trying to be intelligent. Sometimes the best thing for us to do is to be quiet or just to say, "You know what? I don't get it either, but I know that He's going to turn this around."

● ● ●

Repentance is the result of seeing His goodness for what it is.

● ● ●

When somebody has suffered loss, their brain isn't hurting, even though they have questions. It's their heart that's hurting, and so in that context, what we can give is peace. If we have a child who's lost a friend or a parent—tragic, tragic stuff—we can go into the room at night and we can pray for the shalom of Heaven, the peace of God, to permeate everything about them. We saturate our kids with a loving prayer when they're awake but also in their sleep. What this does is put them in a place of safety, where they may have a difficult time processing what's going on, but it's not going to be apart from God. It's going to be with God, and that's what matters.

CHAPTER 27

The Miracle You're Waiting For

How can you become aware of what might be blocking you from receiving your miracle?

BJ: I'm not going to make an assumption that there's a blockage. I don't want to make an assumption because then I'm going to go on a witch hunt. I'm going to try to find something I did wrong. I was in a season of my life where I confessed sins to the Lord that I never committed, just in case it crossed my mind. It became silly. It became so focused on me as the answer that I emphasized something out of its place. The main thing is that He has to speak. This is what I pray: "Lord, I'm in Your Word every day, and I ask You to speak to me. If there's a problem, please use the sword of the Spirit to pierce my own soul, so that even where I might be resistant, God, I give You permission to speak to me. Give me the slap of a friend. Lord, if there's something that I'm not seeing even when I'm reading, bring somebody into my life who will speak honestly to me. Your presence is this consuming fire. Let that glory rest upon me until things change in my heart." That's what I do. I come before the Lord and ask Him to point it out to me. I will repent if I see it. But it's not healthy for me to assume something is wrong with me and that's why there hasn't been a breakthrough. That, to me, starts in the wrong place.

●　●　●

"Your presence is this consuming fire. Let that glory rest upon me until things change in my heart."

●　●　●

You encourage people to avoid introspection. People are trying to figure out what's going on inside them, asking, "What's my problem? What's the other person's problem?" But you're saying simply that God will tell you.

BJ: What happens if you find something? It's not as though you had the ability to fix it, and so it's the wrong place to look. I've never seen anyone become introspective and come out encouraged. Nobody's come out going, "Wow! You should see what I found in here." It's a trick so we stay that way.

● ● ●

I've never seen anyone become introspective and come out encouraged.

● ● ●

CHAPTER 28

LOVING THOSE
WHO MOCK YOU

How have you faced mindsets established within the Church about God being a constant punisher instead of a loving Father guiding, leading and loving us?

BJ: I don't feel the need to change it or correct it. I teach what I teach. It falls on deaf ears. It falls on live ears. It changes the ones who hear and receive, and the ones who are predisposed to resist, they continue for a season. God will get them in another season. I don't feel the need to change or to prove anything. I think the main thing is not just what we teach, but how we live. How do we treat people? How do we treat somebody who has opposed us? What do we do in our corporate gatherings? What do we do as we pray for other churches in town? That's where we speak about the leaders we've met with and know and love who are so diverse and in such different streams. What is our response to all those things that model this heart of God's goodness—this heart we want to live by and illustrate to others? The way we've modeled it is the basis for what we teach, and so that's where it has to go.

•   •   •

The main thing is not just what we teach, but how we live.

•   •   •

But I don't feel the need to change anybody's mind. That's too big of a job, but what I can do is just throw out the message, and if He gives it an expanded platform, then great. If He makes it very small or restricted, it's not a problem. I'm just going to do the best I know how with what He has given me.

CHAPTER 29

PASTORING YOUR FAMILY

How do you relax and make sure you have time for family in the midst of fulfilling your assignment? When you're in a move of God and focused on all those wonderful things, how do you get away and refresh yourself?

BJ: I like spending time with my wife. I get home, and we like to hang out together. We'll sit on the back patio and overlook the beauty, the scenery, have a meal together or coffee and tea or whatever it might be, just to spend time together. You just schedule it. We have a full life, but nobody dictates to us what we do with our time. There's nobody that powerful in any of our lives who can say, "You're on 24/7. You don't have a life." No, I just have to fight for what's important to me, and for me, my family is the first church I pastor. If I don't pastor that "church" well, I don't have the right to pastor another one. We look for time with our kids and grandkids. It may be a meal. It may be a whole day— it may be a year and a half. I took them all to Hawaii last summer. It may be an extended period of time, but you schedule it. It has to be important enough that it attracts your income; it attracts your time, your thought, your emotional investment.

●　●　●

My family is the first church I pastor. If I don't pastor that "church" well, I don't have the right to pastor another one.

●　●　●

CHAPTER 30

Bill Johnson's Top 5 Books

Which five books have most influenced your life and ministry?

BJ: John G. Lake's books in general. *Life and Adventure* by John G. Lake has had great impact on me. I need to read it again. I haven't read it for close to twenty years, but it's such a fabulous book. Rick Joyner has written several books that really impacted me. *The Surpassing Greatness of His Power* had an impact on me. Also, his *Final Quest* series was really impacting. There are just so many of them—I'd have to go to my library and look on my shelf. The one that actually started the change in my life forty-some years ago was *The Normal Christian Life* by Watchman Nee. When I read that I went, "You're kidding? That stuff's in the Bible?" And it made me hungry for the Word. It didn't make me satisfied with other people's writings;

it made me hungry for the Word of God, and that really impacted me a lot. *The Real Faith* by Charles Price—what a classic. Roberts Liardon's *God's Generals*. That really rocked me. When I first read it, I went to the church family at Bethel and said, "This is required reading. You must read this."

What are the top three principles you live by?

BJ: Oh, goodness. It's just loving God well, loving my family well, loving people well. It's just being guided, directed, empowered—just to love well. It's not complicated. There are a lot of complicated things in life, but love isn't. It's sacrificial and giving.

CHAPTER 31

PRAYING FOR YOUR UNBELIEVING CHILD

Do you have any advice for parents stand-ing and praying for their adult kids who were raised in a Christian home but are choosing a different path?

BJ: Obviously, we don't control our kids. What we don't want to do is pick up such a vision and a burden for them that we start manipulating. That's not healthy. What we want to do is call out their destiny whenever we have opportunity. We don't let it be controlling, but we let it be affirmative.

• • •

"Lord, You're the One who set the standard of one lamb per household."

• • •

An acquaintance of mine several years ago would take communion. Their son had just recently cursed them, and it was almost violent, this rejection of the parents. They were in church and taking communion, and they held that cup up before the Lord. The Scriptures say, *"One lamb was sacrificed per household"* (see Exod. 12:3). We hold this before the Lord and say, "Lord, You're the One who set the standard of *one lamb per household*. In other words, everyone in my household is supposed to live under the influence of Your grace, so I remind you of that Word. I declare the power of Your blood to affect my children's lives." We mention their names whenever we pray over them—not out of anxiety, not out of fear, but based on what He has said in his Word. We share and partake of the communion, which is what these people did that Sunday. They hadn't heard from their son in a long time, and the last time they had seen him, he had cursed them and mocked them. But by the time they got home, he called to apologize and repent. Something happened during that communion that turned the heart and brought about real repentance in that child.

Look for creative ways to pray and creative ways to confess God's promises. His promises are stronger than their resistance. It's being anchored in God's ability to work in any situation.

●　●　●

Look for creative ways to pray and creative ways to confess God's promises.

●　●　●

CHAPTER 32

HOSTING THE PRESENCE OF GOD

How do we host His presence wherever we go? How do we align our hearts with Heaven and share the goodness of God with everyone?

BJ: Honestly, it's the whole issue of affection. Just live affectionately aware of Him. It's not like I'm doing something to get breakthrough. I'm not. I'm affectionate toward Him because I love Him—period. If something happens as a result, great. If it's just the fact that I got to walk through this day with my Best Friend ever, that's awesome. Don't make it agenda driven. Make it relational and let Him work out the effects.

• • •

I'm affectionate toward Him because I love Him—period.

• • •

Jesus was baptized in water. When He came up, John said, "*"I saw the Spirit descending from heaven like a dove, and He remained upon Him"* (John 1:32). The whole point was everywhere He went in and through His life, He didn't do anything to spook the dove. A natural dove is a very skittish creature. The way Jesus lived, He didn't violate that presence that was with Him. If you had this dove on your shoulder, how would you walk around the room? Every step would be with the dove in mind. Every movement would be conscious of your wanting to protect His presence, but it isn't because you're afraid of Him abandoning you. It's not a fear thing. It's a respect thing. It's a value; it's affection. That's how it works for me.

For more information on the subject of hosting the presence of God, see *Hosting the Presence* by Bill Johnson.

CHAPTER 33

Closing Prayer

BJ: All we want is to see the Name of Jesus exalted in all of the earth. That's our passion. As the Moravians would pray, we want the Lamb to receive the reward of His suffering. We want Him to be fully honored by nations turning to Him, so we recall Your promise that the news of Your goodness would turn nations. Release over us a Spirit of wisdom and revelation in the knowledge of Him, that You would somehow reveal something to us so deep and profound that it's never shaken again, and that's the truth concerning Your goodness. Establish this truth deep in us to where it becomes what shapes our reaction and our response to a problem. Let it be so profound in its influence that naturally flowing through us are revelation, insight, and actions based on Your kindness and Your goodness. I do pray for this, that Jesus would be exalted, forever praised.

* * *

All we want is to see the Name of Jesus exalted in all of the earth.

* * *

My cry is that You would cause us to become an infectious people—so filled with the conviction of Your goodness that people get it from us. They catch it as a heavenly disease, where we live with this conviction of what You're like. Lord, we want to see the Church change its perspective of Your goodness, and then we want to see the world really come to know how good You are. We pray this, that Jesus would be exalted in all the earth. Amen.

●   ●   ●

We want to see the world really come to know how good You are.

●   ●   ●

ABOUT BILL JOHNSON

Bill Johnson is a fifth-generation pastor with a rich heritage in the Holy Spirit. Bill and his wife, Beni, are the senior leaders of Bethel Church in Redding, California, and serve a growing number of churches that cross denominational lines, demonstrate power, and partner for revival. Bill's vision is for all believers to experience God's presence and operate in the miraculous— as expressed in his bestselling books *When Heaven Invades Earth* and *Hosting the Presence*. The Johnsons have three children and nine grandchildren.

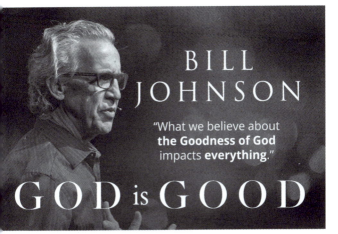

FREE E-BOOKS?
YES, PLEASE!

Get **FREE** and deeply-discounted **Christian books** for your **e-reader** delivered to your inbox **every week!**

IT'S SIMPLE!

VISIT lovetoreadclub.com

SUBSCRIBE by entering your email address

RECEIVE free and discounted e-book offers and inspiring articles delivered to your inbox every week!

Unsubscribe at any time.

SUBSCRIBE NOW!

LOVE TO READ CLUB

visit **LOVETOREADCLUB.COM** ▶